Data

Design

The modern marketers guide to conversion rate optimisation.

By
Al Rowe

Data-Led Design

Written by Al Rowe

Published by

ClickThrough Marketing, UK, 2022

Learn more at

www.clickthrough-marketing.com

and...

https://alrowe.co.uk/

Contents

About the Author	5
Chapter 1: Introduction	7
What is CRO and why is it not enough?	8
How do I know I need to do CRO?	12
Best Practice alone could be a gamble	17
Chapter 2 What is Data-led Design®	19
Data-led Design®	20
Stage One: Data collection and research	29
Stage Two: DATA analysis	36
Stage Three: Design	39
Stage Four: Testing	44
Chapter 3: Being Biased	48
Confirmation bias	50
Framing bias	51
Friendliness bias	53
False consensus bias	54
Negativity bias	56
What user tests are there & how do you conduct them?	57

Chapter 4: User Testing — 57

What users test are there and how do you conduct the? — 58

Chapter 4: 10 Best Practices for high performing conversion — 69

One: The rule of threes — 70

Two: Hide the Navigation on landing pages — 72

Three: Clear, concise headline & sub-heading — 74

Four: Lay out your stall — 75

Five: Explainer videos can have a big effect — 77

Six: Use compelling & relevant supporting imagery — 78

Seven: Make sure key actions are very clear — 79

Eight: Use directional cues or hooks — 81

Nine: Using Conversion-centred Calls to — 84

Ten: Trust factors and social proofs — 87

Final thoughts — 89

References — 92

Acknowledgements — 94

About the Author

I'm Al Rowe, the architect of Data-led Design® and Director of Web Strategy at ClickThrough Marketing, an independent marketing agency which benefits from being technology neutral along with having the status and prestige of being a Google partner. We're able to offer our clients a personalised service while having the flexibility to research and pursue the latest advances in digital marketing. It's due to this that I've been able to focus on what our individual clients' users really need from website improvements, instead of focusing purely on rigid industry wide best practice and expecting to achieve universal results.

I've been with the agency for nearly 10 years now and building websites since 1997. During that time, I have seen how the Internet has exploded and how the websites I built back then would probably be considered mobile friendly now, just because their width was narrower than mobile screens are these days! :)

I have been involved in the production of websites for all types of clients from tiny one-man bands through to larger businesses such as Gtech, Biffa and Helping Hands. I have also always had a keen eye on machine learning and helped create some tech that was the first in the world (as far as I know) to be able to consistently identify clothing types from a photograph.

In the last five years, I have turned my focus to optimizing websites for performance and hitting business goals.

In this book, I will look at why we need to take this idea very seriously and look at how we can push Conversion Rate Optimization a lot further to give our users an improved experience and get superior results.

Chapter 1

-

Introduction

What is CRO and why is it not enough?

CRO stands for Conversion Rate Optimization and is often pronounced 'crow' or 'cee ar oh'. It is an area that has steadily grown since tools like Google Website Optimizer was released in 2007 and adoption and technology have grown substantially ever since. Econsultancy showed in 2017[18] that from 2013 to 2017, only 1% of respondents viewed CRO as not important.

A traditional definition might be: the practice of increasing the percentage of visitors who perform a desired action on a website. This is achieved through tweaking your website and content to generate stronger, higher quality conversions from existing traffic by convincing them to act! But how?

It is not all about conversion rates though, and while improving conversion rates may be a goal, it should not be the only end result, and focussing on it at all may require a different way to measure it.

For example, driving more organic traffic through your blog may reduce your conversion rate since the intent of blog readers may not be transactional. But this doesn't mean that it's advised that you just stop blogging!

To get round this, you could seek to exclude blog traffic from your measurement of conversion rate in order to measure the effects of any other pro-active attempts to drive more conversions.

Another example might be that you pay for a lot of cheap Facebook or display traffic, which again builds the brand but does not lead to many more conversions. Let's imagine you do this only for a period of time - during that time, your sitewide conversion rate will actually look a lot worse. In this case, looking at channel specific conversion rates can help.

If you are actively optimizing for conversion and use a tool like VWO, Optimizely or Google Optimize, then you will probably measure the conversion rate in a much narrower sense to ensure your 'CRO' is working on a page-by-page basis.

So, whilst site-wide conversion rate is not necessarily the right measure, this does not mean that the art and science of Conversion Rate Optimization is invalid. Far from it - in our experience, businesses are more interested in making more money than purely focussing on conversion rates. Consequently, our approach is to **optimize for conversions**. This is a win-win approach.

It is worth recognising that Conversion Rate Optimization ***is not***.....

- Based on guesses.
- Following hunches.
- Copying what everyone else is doing.

- Driven by the highest paid person's opinion (HiPPO).

In fact, Conversion Rate Optimization should be based on only one set of people's opinions - the users of your site. By listening to the data, following how they interact with your brand, and drilling it down to some cold hard facts, you'll remove guesswork and ensure you have clear processes in place that eliminate room for personal opinions, whether from HiPPOs or an entire safari of stakeholders!

Who is doing conversion marketing?

Although Econsultancy[18] showed in 2017 that 50% of respondents consider CRO crucial to their overall digital marketing strategy, ConversionXL[19] found in 2016 that 68% of small businesses do not have a documented or structured CRO strategy.

By 2018 this was 63%[20]. So a move in the right direction but still a long way to go. Hubspot[21] found in 2020 that only 17% of marketers use Landing Page A/B testing to improve conversion rates. And yet Marketing Sherpa[22] found that 74% of Conversion Optimization programs increase sales.

We know from our experience that it is one of most powerful tools in our Digital Marketing armoury when done right, so consider it a substantial mistake to ignore it.

How do I know I need to do CRO?

If any of the following are true, then you should consider optimizing for conversion:

- You get lots of traffic but very few sales or leads.
- You do not know where people drop off in the funnel.
- Consumer psychology is new to you.

- Your website still looks the same as when you made it.
- You are in the process of rebuilding your site.
- Your customers are complaining they cannot do what they want on your site.

Conversion killers are everywhere

There are many reasons why your website may not be reaching its full potential and why you may not be getting the business you want or deserve.

A few of the biggest contributors are:

- Poor load speed.
- Poor on page experience (covers a lot).
- User confidence.
- Limited payment options.
- Poor 'add to cart' buttons.
- Poor checkout or form fill experience.

- Poor payment pages.

There are also many other, sometimes off-site factors that can affect your site performance. Sometimes these heavily skew your website's performance and can make measurement really difficult. These include:

- Price competitiveness.
- Brand reputation.
- Stock availability.
- Amazon.
- A slow web development cycle.
- HiPPOs (Highest Paid Person's Opinion).

So, how do you do CRO?

In simple terms, you could take a look at a page and if you feel it could be better, you could decide to do something about it. You could design and then create something you hope is better and then replace the current page with your new version. If conversions go up, you could argue that your improvement has made all the difference and solved the problem.

You may be right. But you may be wrong. There could be a whole host of onsite or offsite reasons why there is now an improvement. You cannot prove it was your new version. Also, what happens if you get less conversions? How do you know that what you are doing is right? How do you know what needs changing?

In the above scenario, there are a LOT of assumptions. This is why we need a methodology.

This is why we tend to split (or A/B) test. Testing is a more scientific way of proving that one version or another is superior. It allows us to gain statistical data and show with different degrees of certainty that one or another version is genuinely better than the other. This all depends on how you define your goals.

To do this, we typically use software. Some notable solutions are:

- Google Optimize.
- VWO (formerly Visual Website Optimizer).
- Optimizely.
- AB Tasty.

There are loads of others too, all with different pricing models to suit different target markets.

In essence these allow you to conduct the following tests:

- Split URL.
- True A/B.
- Multivariate.

- Multi Arm Bandit.

They all have one thing in common. They all test on your live traffic.

So how do we arrive at a solution that is superior?

Well, there are two main ways. We use best practice to steer our design changes. We use offline user-testing to steer our designs. Data-led Design® is about combining both of these approaches.

Best Practice alone could be a gamble

Traditional CRO relies heavily on best practice for success. A few of my favourites are in the last section.

The problem with best practice alone is that it doesn't always work. Sometimes it works better in some verticals than others, but exactly when and where it works is difficult to predict. This is why we test. However, depending on how you arrived at what you think will be an improvement, when you conduct a split test you may be effectively gambling with your traffic.

On some sites this might be ok. But on a high-performing ecommerce site, the difference can be noticeable. In my experience, people responsible for eCommerce websites are a lot closer to their performance data and know down to the day and sometimes hour how well their site is doing.

This is why we need to do everything we can to ensure that any tests we run improve things. So, how can you improve your tests?

Use Data-led Design® of course!

Chapter 2

-

What is Data-led Design®?

Data-led Design®

As the name suggests - uses data to inform design decisions. It is the unique combination of the traditional principles of Conversion Rate Optimization married to a market research approach using offline user-testing. It is an approach to improving universal user experience aside from any nuances of any one industry or business niche.

We define it as a continuous process used to produce optimal designs, informed by data available at the time of creation. It combines existing data sources with offline user tests. Depending on the problem we are trying to solve or the goal we have set determines what data sources we need and what tests we should run. It also determines which areas of the site we should focus on.

Once test results have been collected, they are then analysed for consistent actionable feedback and the process continues with a new optimal design being created. If no further useful feedback is collected at this time, the process for this element has come to a conclusion - the optimal design has been achieved.

It can be used to optimize existing online assets such as web pages but also can be much wider to include visual adverts, copy, landing pages, apps. It can also be used as a process to create new web sites. *For the purposes of simplicity, I am mostly going to discuss websites in this book. But, remember the principles apply much more broadly.*

The reason we created this methodology was because, as an agency, we've been working with clients on website evolution, new websites and SEO site migrations for years. Throughout this time, we sat through meeting after meeting as clients completely overhauled their design because 'it's in need of a refresh'.

Sometimes, the new websites our clients created did not perform better on launch (some of us remember Myspace!). They may have looked better, but they did not perform better.

We realised this was because many agencies just created the website they thought the business wanted or needed. No-one actually thought about how the current website was performing or why it was performing in the way it was. This meant that a company deciding they needed a new website was actually a very risky time for them, whether they knew it or not.

We can learn from the way that companies like Facebook or the BBC release major updates to their platforms. They communicate to and involve their users to gain feedback and minimise user disruption.

If you do it right, the next version of your digital asset could fly instead of sink.

The way we market has changed and with this, so has the way we need to craft our online experience. It's no longer just about creating something that looks good. We need to ensure that the user can find exactly what they need, in the fastest time possible.

We had also noticed that making new websites just wasn't as much fun as it used to be. This was in part because most of the time, each website we made was the nth generation for the company and that their business had now come to rely on it as a key business channel. Of course, as time has gone on and particularly due to the pandemic, this has become ever more true.

So, we realised that unless we could guarantee that performance would be better, we were in for trouble.

Over the last few years, we have sought to get the very best results for our customers and that means ongoing gains, and it also means that individual tests should not generate negative results. Ever!

This is one of the reasons why we created Data-led Design®. Put simply, Data-led Design® is like CRO on steroids. Data-led Design® is our unique methodology to evolve web and landing pages to maximize desired behaviour. It is not an alternative to CRO but works to make it better. Much, much better!

The fact of the matter is that best practice design is not enough. Online testing is not enough.

Data-led Design® is an approach to using user-data to steer and influence our design and test decisions and with it we have made serious, provable money for our clients.

It is important to understand though, that we still love visuals, we still love creativity, but we *really* love data.

Creativity + data = magic

Data-Led Design® can provide assurances that investments are being made on change that is beneficial. Analysis of current data, considering known pain points, setting SMART goals to test hypotheses and arming yourself with a hit-list that prioritises actions allows you to completely trust where your budget is spent.

Who said data couldn't be sexy?
Data-led Design® is the sweet spot between creative design and data driven UX optimization.

It is also a better business model because it works best when you do it continuously.

We have found with several clients that over months of the process, we can return to the home page, say six or twelve months later and still make fantastic gains. This is because the world is always changing, people are always changing, UX trends, technological advances, prices, demand etc. are always changing.

Therefore, a forward thinking business should always be testing. All we can do is seek to improve on the current state of play.

We can learn from the past, but we can never return to it and there are always reasons why the future will be different.

Data-led Design® has been transformative to our agency and there is still a distance to travel to get the most out of its logic. We are a conversion-centric agency and conversion is at the heart of everything we do.

So, how does it work in practice?

It consists of four stages; **data collection, data analysis, design and then testing**. These stages can equally apply to a traditional CRO approach where you seek to understand how the site is performing then create online split tests to aim to get better results.

Whilst running tests, you then collect data on how your variants are performing. You analyse this, then make adjustments and re-test. This is called cycle testing.

With Data-led Design®, before we begin online split tests, we undertake a rigorous approach to offline user-testing. It is this understanding that makes this process more like 'super CRO'.

Regardless of whether you undertake offline user tests, the best way to work out how to make an improvement, is to understand the current situation.

The four stages of data-led design

01. Data Collection

Real user data is collected specific to your business, from a variety of sources. This includes data from Analytics, heatmaps and user testing.

02. Data Analysis

The data collected helps us understand your user's mindset and behaviour verses expectations. This analysis is the foundation for an improved design and UX.

04. Testing

Usability testing provides qualitative feedback which cannot be gathered through data alone. This helps to build a more complete picture

03. Design

A design is produced which is not only led by data but abides by UX and conversion best practise. This combined approach produces the optimal design

Stage One: Data collection and research

Using any data source we can, we learn as much as possible about current performance. This might be GA, it might be Hotjar, it might be talking to your sales teams and other stakeholders. If none are available we may install tools to start us off. However, be mindful, every tool slows the site down and site speed is a big conversion killer.

There are many ways to understand your current traffic and behaviour. For us this usually starts with analysing data a business already has. This is usually Google or Adobe Analytics. Look for things like:

- How conversion rates have changed, across the board and by segment.
- How mobile has changed. Has the split changed, has the mobile conversion rate changed?

- Has the way you are driving traffic changed? I.e. the channel split

- Have the pages that people visit changed (in UA: Behavior->Site Search->All pages)?

- Have the search terms (in UA: behavior->Site Search->Search Terms) changed over time? This may reflect changes in user intent as well as product or service priority changes.

- In Google's UA, you can also use the navigation analysis to see if the page journeys have changed over time.

It is also very useful to look at high level metrics such as bounce rate, session duration, sessions and pages per user.

In *GA4* (Google Analytics 4) engagement is a very useful metric.

Getting the most out of your analytics package for the purposes of optimizing for conversion is a whole other topic but a few things you will definitely want to look at are:

- Goals
- Events
- Funnels

All of these take proactive setting up rather than the defaults mentioned above. GA4, being Google's cookieless analytics offering, is all about events rather than sessions (since these rely on cookies). You get some events by default such as click and scroll.

However to really get the most out of it, you will want to understand how users should or do use your site and set up specific events to be able to analyse those journeys properly.

There are a whole host of CRO tools available. Many, many, many more than you will need. There are lists of them online if you want to find new ones. We tend to use some key ones a LOT more than others. They fall into certain categories which include:

- Session videos.
- User polls.
- Heat maps.

Be mindful of GDPR or equivalent which may prevent some being allowed on your site.

Session Videos

We tend to use *Hotjar* for all of these but have used others including *Crazyegg* and *Sessioncam*. Seeing what users do takes time as you physically sit through a video watching what they do and trying to spot where things might be going wrong.

Things to look out for with session recordings are:

- Short recordings may show you the disinterested or those experiencing issues.

- Longer recordings will show a full user journey (or someone that went for a cup of tea or to receive a parcel).

It can be a useful way to see the site through the user's eyes. If you see something broken, fix it.

User Polls

There are many tools that allow you to create polls on your website. We mostly use Hotjar for this. In Hotjar there are two types; feedback and surveys.

We find up to 10% of users may complete a Feedback popout, registering views at the extremes. Though not indicative of the general user, these can yield important insights.

Surveys are the polls where you can ask single or conditional questions to try to get an answer on something specific. Be careful not to introduce biases into your questions. These are useful to deal with specific concerns but can get spammy results..

Heatmaps

Heatmaps are probably the most useful tool for understanding on-page behaviour and indicating how it might need to change.

Again, we tend to use *Hotjar* mostly for heatmaps but also like *Crazyegg* (which has improved a lot recently). VWO, our preferred split testing tool also does heatmaps but we just seem to get more out of Hotjar's.

Things to look out for on a heat map are:

- High clicked elements.
- Low clicked elements.

- Scroll depth.
- Is one element distracting?
- Is an element that drives business low on interaction?
- Are there unanticipated clicked elements?

Sales teams and other stakeholders

Sometimes the best information can come from sales teams or chat operatives. This is because this group are used to dealing with buyer questions and problems in the buyer journey.

Often the information they possess is not on the website and they get asked the same thing over and over again.

These questions can be fundamental to buyer friction. By learning about these, we can factor this into changes to copy or design of new elements.

Stage Two: DATA analysis

Through analysing these data sources we can build up a picture about how key pages or sections of a page are performing. We look for low hanging fruit, areas that obviously look wrong or are probably failing. But we also look for other issues deeper in the journey.

We often take the approach of using the funnel to guide us, starting with the home page, then progressing to service or category pages, then to individual services or product pages through to lead capture forms or the checkout process.

If the checkout process is the most obvious problem then we prioritise this.

We usually do this top down on the basis that if you can open the sluice gate on traffic blockers, you can drive more conversions. Sometimes though you may have issues at checkout that are causing huge drop-offs and naturally become the priority.

How you prioritise is a question of balancing potential rewards from change against cost of execution.

Sometimes high implementation costs are worth it. Working with Waste Management giant Biffa, during their digital transformation phase, we used Data-led Design® to rebuild their site. As part of our data collection phase it became clear that users wanted to understand what business pricing looked like and get a quote for their different services. At the time, there was no mechanism to do this beyond a fairly buried, complicated long form. Designing and creating this was a substantial project in its own right. Before starting, we looked at the demand, looked at the current form fills and looked at the potential return on investment to make the business case. It was clear that creating this had huge potential, could be extremely important even if it wasn't going to be easy.

The release of this new feature and its placement front and centre on the homepage led to a 50% increase in conversions. The project paid for itself on day one and after the first month had generated a very significant increase in sales.

However, we determine what areas of a site might need improvement, we create a hit list of potential areas and record these in a Kanban (VWO has its own, but we also use Trello). At this stage we also create a number of SMART goals to set ourselves some KPIs or targets to hit. This may be to demonstrate return on investment or to meet business needs.

A few typical aims we might set smart goals from are:

- Increase phone calls.

- Generate more form fills.
- Generate more relevant form fills.
- Increase sales.
- Send more traffic down the funnel.
- Better explain the value proposition.

Stage Three: Design

This, along with testing is where the magic happens. This is where we combine the outcomes of our data analysis with our experience and known best practices. Exactly how we approach the design depends entirely on what we have learned and the extent to which the different data sources are available. It also depends on the outcomes of our user tests.

For example, if we are evolving a lead generation site where phone calls are the lifeblood of the business and the number of phone calls appears to have dropped. The first question to ask is, how are you recording phone calls? Ideally, anything you want to improve needs to be measurable, how else can you get any data?

So for phone calls, some form of call tracking such as Google's own, *ResponseTap* or *Infinity Call Tracking* makes life a lot easier. If the website is mostly viewed on mobile then you may be able to measure taps on the phone number as a goal. However, if these things are not in place, then you are left with **hearsay** or anecdotal evidence. This unfortunately happens too often!

Let's assume, we can measure and monitor the key behaviours or goals we want to improve. In these cases, we can create new design variants to target those specific aims and then, when ready, test against this for improvement.

The key differentiator in Data-led Design® is that we do not just design and then online-test. ***Instead, we use offline user-testing to inform and then iterate designs until we have no further actionable insights.*** More on this later.

How do we create new designs?

Having decided on the first area to redesign, the next thing to be mindful of is the client's brand guidelines. It is important that any changes made are sympathetic to the overall balance of the site (unless we are hypothesising that the current overall aesthetic is no longer working).

There are a lot of factors that may need to be considered to arrive at what we hope will be an optimal design and this includes:

- What problem we are trying to solve, which page it is on and where on the page
- If there are any other contributing factors, such as ensuring continuity of

language with the previous step to meet visitor expectations

- Whether the language itself is working as hard as it can to achieve the goal. There is a whole art to the psychology of persuasion.

- Whether we can bring any specific previous experience to inform decisions

Best Practice is a good starting point

As a general rule, we factor in best practices and use a checklist which covers 60 key questions and covers such things as:

- Overall messaging.
- Conversion-centred design.
- Form design.
- Usability.
- Urgency and scarcity (FOMO).

- Trust and authority.
- Value proposition.
- Social proofing and similarity.
- Choice paralysis.
- Friction.
- Reciprocity.
- Fulfilment anxiety.
- After sales service.

How we judge the above is quite subjective and consequently, is only a guide. Not all are relevant to all situations either. Every detail counts and it is easy to jump to inaccurate conclusions or think you know best.

A word of warning, however. With all design best practices, how well they work depends on many factors including how well they are executed but also how popular they are. This may differ per industry.

For example, in the contract vehicle purchase market, we have seen evidence that some visitors are not fooled by 'people like me' images while others were actively put off by the use of a celebrity endorsement. That said, a number of user testers also felt that they trusted the website more because of the celebrity ambassador. It shows why testing is so vital!

Stage Four: Testing

Some of us may have been AB split testing but online testing is not enough!

The real reason Data-led Design® gets great results is because of the impact learnings from offline user-testing can have to help influence designs.

So having used our experience and knowledge of best practice, analysed all the data points we can and learned as much as we can about the website we are working on, we created our hitlist. From this we then created a first draft design solution. No matter how much we try to be impartial, any designer is only human. It is inevitable that we will have introduced our own biases either consciously, out of habit or subconsciously into the design. We will cover this in more detail in the section on biases later.

To help combat our biases, we use a combination of offline user-testing techniques to interrogate our assumptions. The purpose is to learn from potential website visitors how a design will be received and more accurately, predict how it will perform in the virtual world.

It is only through testing that we can know that what we are doing is working. User-testing is all about asking the right questions.

Again we will run through some of the options for user testing in a later section.

Traditionally, user testing is only used to help understand the current situation. With Data-led Design® we do a series of iterative offline user tests. If the first attempt at a new design does not perform as well as we expect or if there are reasons why the original is still preferred, we take any learnings and iterate the design.

After each round of user testing, you may be equipped to ask more questions. In some cases you will have *some* evidence to make changes to your design.

With each iteration, you then test again, examining the changes you have made. In practice, this may involve two to five iterations.

When we feel that we are no longer gaining any actionable insights, we determine that the optimum design has been reached. In this case we would then proceed to set up an online AB test to investigate how the new design performs against the original, in the (real) virtual world.

Chapter 3

-

Being Biased

What biases should I avoid?

In this section we will look at some of the main biases we want to minimise.

Since we are going to be asking different questions in our user tests, it makes sense to look at potential biases first.

The main forms of bias[17] we look out for are:

1. Confirmation bias
2. Framing bias
3. Friendliness bias
4. False consensus bias
5. Negativity bias

Again, there are whole books on this. The purpose is to consider how to ask the right questions through minimising biases.

Confirmation bias

This is when you have your own idea and then try to make the data fit to it (rather than interpreting based solely on the data).

We could ask a question like *'Do you think the red call to action stands out?'*

The problem with this is that the phrasing led respondents not to provide negative or opposing feedback. We are leading our audience and forcing them to consciously become aware of the call to action button and its redness. We are bringing out own suspicions here and influencing respondents.

What we really want is to observe natural behaviour to determine if it furthers our aim.

A better way to find out what stands out is to ask a question like *'what would you click on next?'*

The more diverse the users you have, the more perspectives you will receive. So we want to avoid leading questions.

You could ask *'did the wide variety of products available make it difficult to find the specific product you wanted?'*.

This phrasing led respondents to perceive that finding a product was difficult in the first place. A simply, less biased way to phrase this is: *'did you have any difficulty finding the product you wanted? If so, why?'*

Framing bias

I think of this a bit like political spin. It all depends on how you interpret results and what conclusions you make because of that.

In 2016 the Nielsen Norman Group[16] tested 1037 UX professionals. They asked the question *'Should a search function be redesigned, based on usability testing findings?'*.

They then told 50% (let's call them group A) that 4 out of 20 users did not find the search function and 50% (group B) that 6 out of 20 users found the search function.

The results were interesting. They showed that 51% of group A said yes, it should be redesigned to make it easier to find. Only 39% of group B said that.

This showed that those shown the negative interpretation (group A) were 31% more likely to believe that redesign was necessary. Group A were more influenced to consider the poor 4 out of 20 users who struggled rather than the 16 who did not.

A consequence of framing bias is that you can get a clustering illusion, which is perceiving patterns that are actually coincidence. Also, people tend to weight by order, which means they give more weight to the first piece of data. These mental traps influence design decisions.

Whilst interpreting user test results, it is important to see things from all angles. Great, 70% of respondents feel the UX is intuitive….BUT…not so great, 30% do not. What conclusions would you draw?

Friendliness bias

This occurs when familiarity means that people tell you what they think you want to hear. It is the principle of least effort. When a friend or colleague asks you a challenging question, how easy is it to just confirm or reassure that everything is fine, when secretly you harbour feelings that this is not true?

With user-testing, this occurs most commonly with face-to-face focus groups. The way round this is to try to:

- Ensure the testers do not know you
- Ensure the testers know what is expected of them

- not ask them too much, keep them focussed and motivated

We get around this by always using blind testing.

False consensus bias

This is the assumption that others think the same way as you do. Social media algorithms have famously shown this with highly polarising results. If the algorithm detects you think a certain way, you will be shown more and more posts that support this viewpoint. This leads you to the sometimes-false conclusion that everyone feels the same way as you.

This has a positive reinforcement effect on your psychology, empowering you to confidently assert your viewpoint. Your friends then show friendliness bias, making the least effort and do not necessarily challenge. This then confirms your view further and bolsters the cycle.

In testing, it is important to interrogate your questions. It can help by honestly writing down your own opinions, assumptions and potential prejudices. Then with this in mind ask if your questions are favouring your own viewpoint.

The purpose of user-testing is to bring new viewpoints into the mix, not to confirm your own thoughts. This has always been a historic problem for scientists who struggle to let go of their theories even with strong evidence against them.

Negativity bias
I find this one of the most interesting of the biases. Humans are evolved towards self-preservation. Something going wrong is a much bigger deal than something going right.

If you have done a good job with your design and people generally approve of it as well as find using it easy then you may find you get a lot less meaningful feedback. You may find testers seem more unusually obsessed with any areas that are sub-optimal at the expense of you being able to conclude that in most areas all is well.

This is a really tricky judgement call and ultimately brings subjectivity back into play. If on analysing feedback, you feel that the potential impact of anything negative is minimal but that is the only meaningful feedback you have, then will have to decide to what extent you act. It is the job of subsequent design iterations and tests to interrogate this further.

You can minimise this by using best practices and ensuring designs use known conventions and standards and by designing neutral questions that draw attention to the negative areas highlighted.

It is important though, to not allow what does not work to overwhelm your design process.

Chapter 4

-

User Testing

What user tests are there and how do you conduct them?

In this section we will look at some of the user testing methods available as there are a number of different ways to conduct user tests. This may be through using people you know, such as colleagues. You could recruit people from a target audience and run a face to face or virtual focus group. There are also online platforms that offer blind user testing. There are some similarities between user testing and market research and so business.yougov.com is worth a look. There are plenty of other platforms out there such as:

- Usertesting.com
- Userlytics.com

- Userfeel.com
- Userbrain.com
- Usabilityhub.com

We have used a few of these but mostly use *Usabilityhub*. With the best platforms you will have the ability to filter your testing audience by things like:

- Device to be tested.
- Tester location.
- Age.
- Gender.
- Employment status.
- Income.
- I.T. literacy.
- Interest areas.

The sorts of tests we conduct are:

- Context questioning session recordings.
- 5 second flash tests.
- First click tests.
- Navigation tests.
- Preference tests.

It is important to note that offline user testing is not the same as AB testing, nor is it a replacement. It is however the stage which, if done right ensures that your online AB tests have a better chance of succeeding. This is particularly true if you are trying to make larger changes such as redesigning the whole hero area of the home page.

Whatever user testing you do, it is important to try to gather quantitative information as well as qualitative. You cannot hope to gain statistical significance if you do not have a sufficient sample size.

However, there is always a compromise between gaining useful insights and budgets. Key questions can be answered through numbers and quantitative information. People's opinions then provide potential reasons. We never act on people's opinions alone, unless several people say the same thing.

Context questioning session recordings

If you want to learn how current websites are navigated or how people arrive at decisions to take action on a website, using the likes of usertesting.com can help. You pay for each person who records a video. Some people do this to earn extra cash and there are scammers to avoid. I have only had good results.

The key to getting useful information here is to ask the right questions. You may need to do a few rounds of this to get sufficiently useful information, or else you may need to use other tests first to enable designing the right set of tasks or questions.

In the first instance you want to understand the general view the audience has of the usability of the site and whether there are any obvious issues requiring immediate attention.

Assuming you have deduced (often this can be concluded from Google Analytics alone,) what the key user journeys are, you may then set users the task of completing a particular journey.

For example, a couple of years ago, we conducted research for Dunelm to look at their 'made to measure' curtains in contrast to Hillarys Blinds. Having looked at the URLs involved in the purchase of made to measure curtains, we ran a series of usability videos to compare this journey with Hillarys Blinds.

When using a platform to run tests, we cannot guarantee we genuinely have recruited suitable participants. You may have an understanding of the right target audience from analytics data or sales data or simply through knowing your business so well and you may have evolved personas.

More often than not, tester audiences are only an approximation to this and so this evidence is only a steer; it is not as good as a real audience.

Because of this you need to give context to any questions asked to ensure you give your testers the best chance of being helpful. So in this example, it may be something like:

'You are in the process of decorating your lounge and are actively considering buying made-to-measure curtains. You are new to this and want to learn more.

Navigate through this website to find information to help you understand the process. Verbalise your thinking as you progress. Once you have found out the process works, progress to the next task.'

Later they will then see a follow up task: *'you are now ready to make an appointment, navigate to do this. Complete the process and explain your thoughts as you progress through each stage. Please do not actually book an appointment.'*

This is repeated for each of the websites (in this case Dunelm and Hillarys Blinds). The questions are deliberately open but give enough context and instruction.

These videos were extremely important in highlighting the key differences between the two sites' approach and a sense of user preferences. We only used three videos, so any information provided was not statistically significant. However, it provided enough useful opinions to design other tests to interrogate the themes more deeply.

Five second flash tests

Five second flash tests can be very useful in learning if an audience understands what a design or web page is for. It can help you to see if users immediately get it. It is about first impressions.

In practice, you provide testers with between 3 and 20 seconds to see a visual and ask key questions. You may ask questions like:

- What brand was this for?
- What can you remember about this business?
- What does this business do?
- What words do you remember from this business?
- Do you find this business to be trustworthy?

First click tests

Another tool to learn about first impressions, the first click test is useful to learn if users can quickly complete a task. It is also to see if users can see correctly what is clickable. It usually consists of a task, the user clicking and then follow up questions.

Questions for this sort of test will depend heavily on what problem you are trying to solve but may be things like:

- Where would you click to get in touch?
- Where would you click to see new products?
- Where would you click to add to basket?
- You are on a mobile, where would you click to call?

Follow up questions may ask for a confidence level or feeling of easiness.

Navigation tests

This is a useful test to find out if users can find the right actions to complete a multi-step process and also if users can correctly determine what is clickable.

Questions might be things like:

- You wish to download an ebook, how do you do this?
- You wish to sign up for a business bank account, how do you do this?
- You are looking for a biology course, how do you find this?

Preference tests

This is the test we probably use the most often. It is closest to AB tests in execution, though has a different purpose.

With this test, users are shown two or more alternative designs and asked key questions such as:

- Which design do you prefer?
- Which website would you buy from?
- Which website do you find easiest to use?
- Which website do you trust the most?

The first provides a percentage outcome (quantitative). In each case, follow up questions are useful to qualify choices.

This provides qualitative information.

- Please explain your choice.
- Why did you make this choice? Please explain your reasons.

Preference tests are useful for:

- Comparing current designs against competitors.
- Comparing new designs against currently live designs (this could be a site redesign or just an evolutionary step).

Chapter 5

-

10 Best Practices for high performing conversion

User testing and the methodology outlined here for Data-led Design® will radically improve your results but it all assumes you know the basics of good UX and some design best practices. There are many books covering this. In this final section I am just going to run through a few that we use time and time again to help us think about laying out and organising our content. There is no guarantee they will work for every client but they are a great way to start in creating your variations for testing.

Supporting images for this section can be found at https://alrowe.co.uk/data-led-design-book-supporting-images/

Best practice one:
The rule of threes

It should be no surprise that all the recent slogans released by the UK government always consist of three parts such as *'catch it, bin it, kill it'* or *'stay home, protect the NHS, save lives'.*

This is because someone in the government is well aware of the rule of threes. This is everywhere. It's as easy as 1,2,3 or a,b,c or bronze, silver, gold. There's a reason.

If you have ever done a memory test, you will be told that most people are able to remember up to 7 (plus or minus 2) things in their head at once. This comes from a psychology paper by George Miller in 1956[15]. It is almost certain, however, that everyone can remember 3.

The concept of 'over-choice' was first introduced by Alvin Toffler[14] in 1970, though others have failed to replicate his findings. This feeds into a narrative called 'choice paralysis'. An interesting study on Jam samples was published by Professor Sheena Iyengar, who showed that with two jam sampling stations, one featuring 24 jams resulted in only 3% making a purchase compared to the other featuring only 6 jams which led to 30% of samplers making a purchase.

So, we might be able to handle 5-9 but 3 just seems about right.

In 2014 Unbounce[13] published their findings that reducing choices from 4 to 3 increased conversions by 16.93%.

The rule of threes can be useful all over a website, but can be overused. You could use it:

- To demonstrate a beginning, middle and end of a narrative
- To show 3 USPs
- To provide 3 product or service choices
- To show 3 customer benefits
- To show 3 testimonials etc

**Best Practice Two:
Hide the Navigation on landing pages**

If you have managed to craft a coherent user-journey starting with paid advertising through to a landing page and there is a discrete and simple offer, it can be useful to make life easy for visitors by removing the main navigation.

This again is connected to choice paralysis.

In these situations, we are really not offering any choice and also do not want the user to go off anywhere else. This is quite an old fashioned, strong arm tactic but we still find it works.

Shopify (and HubSpot) still use it on their landing pages and you can see it on almost any decent checkout process. This ensures the user does not lose focus and can only really complete their purchase at the moment of truth.

Best Practice Three:
Clear, concise headline and sub-heading

In 1903, Elias. St. Elmo Lewis[12], laid out his advertising principles and stated:

'The mission of an advertisement is to attract a reader, so that he will look at the advertisement and start to read it; then to interest him, so that he will continue to read it; then to convince him, so that when he has read it he will believe it. If an advertisement contains these three qualities of success, it is a successful advertisement.'

The rule of threes is at play here again, but with our increasingly diminished attention spans caused by freedom of choice and increasing competition across the entire internet, it has never been harder to keep someone's attention. Are you even still reading this?[1]

Using a clear headline hopefully will grab their attention, the sub-heading then sucks them in and the call to action that follows should encourage them to dig deeper.

Best Practice Four: Lay out your stall

Again using the rule of threes can help, but using some structure lay out your stall. This might be:

- Further value statements
- Sentences or bullet points that clearly state what the offer includes and why (they all make a difference)
- Try to anticipate customer questions

Some of the best performing product landing pages use a longer, more luxurious sell, rich with video and imagery. This is particularly used in decent technology landing pages.

Apple are the master here. But it could and arguably should be used for any considered purchase such as holidays and cars. With this model, no detail is too small. It is all about knowing what your audience want. How do you find this out? Test!

This is where the information gleaned from chat operatives or sales staff can be very useful. Any frequently repeated customer concerns or questions can be answered in well written copy or an FAQ section.

Laying out the stall might be the content to describe a product, or it maybe how you explain your business to newcomers. Always remember to consider what's in it for the customer.

It may be about:

- Teaching users about your services?

- Teaching users how to use your products?

- About a free trial or saving money

Best Practice Five:
Explainer videos can have a big effect

I find getting videos to work well is not as easy as I think it should be. However, when we have important information to communicate, particularly when using pictures can help, videos are a great way to increase engagement.

Generation Z are brought up on YouTube and if it is not a video, what is the point? Even some of us Millennials find it easier to consume content through video than any other form.

Wyzowl[13] found in 2019 that 87% of their respondents wished to see more videos from brands that year. YouTube found that 50% of generation Z and Millennials 'couldn't live without video'. How would they cope?

A strong video not only useful for getting a message across, also shows you are serious and as a result consumers may take you more seriously for having video content.

However, as mentioned, placement and position is important. Often, expensive video is buried on a site down where no-one scrolls.

You may need to use design to make a strong feature out of your video (like the example above) and working out where is best on the site takes testing.

Best Practice Six:
Use compelling and relevant supporting imagery

Even if you are selling digital products or services, often less is more and careful use of images can communicate more strongly than more words. (Granted you may still want those words for SEO!)

This may be the cover of an ebook for the lead gen form capture of a premium piece of content download, it could be a screenshot of a webinar or video, product or service or maybe it is a graphic design incorporating your offer.

Finding some imaginative way to visualise something intangible, can make it seem like the user is going to get something...well....tangible.

Best Practice Seven:
Make sure key actions are very clear (and NEVER say 'submit')

Whatever behaviour you are trying to encourage, make sure you make it easy for a user to do this. If you want more phone calls, make it very clear how people can call.

If you want more form fills, then include a clear button linking to that form, or include the form at the right place in the journey.

Make sure the button copy is meaningful such as '**download your ebook**', '**sign up for free**'.

After ensuring the button text was meaningful on the previous stage, they have left it as '**Submit**' on the actual form. This is lazy. Submit also carries with it a sense of subservience which can be off-putting.

Again, testing can help optimize the best copy for your situation.

When it comes to forms, there is a lot of published best practice out there. Consider the number of fields you collect. This can influence both the quantity and quality of form fills you receive and again, testing helps get this balance right. In the days of a post-GDPR world, we also need to be mindful of data protection and data privacy should be made clear at the point of submission

Best Practice Eight:
Use directional cues or hooks

In the old days we would have an image point directly to the button but in these days of uber-competition and data protection, users are less likely to give you their email address without understanding why. The example below uses a finger and arm to point to the heading which encourages us to read and hopefully complete the form.

When using images of people, always avoid images that use or suggest direct eye contact. This seems backwards to what we know about trust building. There is something primal at looking into another's eyes. The problem is that you can get lost in them. In the case above, you might spend more time looking into the model's eyes and get distracted so as not to follow the direction to read the words.

Instead, you want to us *eye line* as a directional cue. So that if we look at the man's face on a landing page, readers will more likely look to where *his eyes* are pointing and follow that line of sight and which will hopefully be some snappy text and nice juicy button to click.

This is one of the oldest tricks in the book, so to speak.

Imagine a world where there are no signposts on the road....yes and you have no SatNav app on your phone. Difficult to imagine isn't it? Imagine how lost you would get. On the motorways sometimes you still take a wrong turn even with directions and signposts.

Unsurprisingly, websites are no different. Remember, they are not books where we can read pages sequentially. We need to make it clear to users how they do things.

If we want to encourage people to do something in particular to hit a marketing goal, then we have to do extra work to make that happen and clear signposts and directional cues help here. The oldest tricks work the best.

These can take several forms. Arrows can be very subtle but effective in directing users. It is about considering pathways and lines of sight. Arrows can be used for different purposes.

Sometimes they are used to indicate that something is a clickable button. They can also suggest that someone reads something. In the example below, the arrow encourages the user to read the words 'see how it works'. Because of the border, it still looks clickable so the arrow both helps to indicate a button and encourage reading. So often, you will see the arrow to the right of the text, which does not quite have the same effect.

My favourite example of this can be found on the strange website *pantsandsocks.com*[10]. As the cursor moves over a large, bold block of red, a video starts to play.

A cheeky and slightly self-conscious male model - in just a pair of red pants - points playfully over at the *subscribe* button. Genius (it made me click it!).

Best Practice Nine:
Using Conversion-centred Calls to Action *(and yes, Buttons)*

This is about knowing your audience and understanding good usability. It is about use of colour, spacing and layout. It is about using a number of different content delivery mechanisms and formatting styles to break content up and prevent the user getting bored.

Ask yourself if your design is clear and uncluttered. Good conversion centred design should enable a user to easily scan the page and immediately know what it is about (ideally in less than 5 seconds).

Think carefully about colours. Ideally you are able to recognise the different levels of buttons you have on the site. There will be one behaviour which should be classed as your *Primary Call To Action* (CTA). This may be the *'buy'* button or *'download'* or *'get in touch'* as opposed to *'learn more'* or *'view course'*.

The primary CTA should use a colour **not used anywhere else** on the site. It should stand out.

All buttons of the same sort should use this style so it becomes established in the visitor's mind as important.

There are no hard and fast best practices with button colours, some work better on certain sites and a colour that works for one company is not guaranteed to work on another. This will be partly to do with how that colour sits in context of your brand colours.

It is worth recognising that different colours have different temperatures and evoke a different subliminal emotion. We usually find that the complementary but contrasting brand colour works best.

Occasionally, we do tap into the psychology of colours and may use say red for danger or green for calm, blue for trust etc.

Susan Weinschenk in her book; *Neuro Web Design: What Makes Them Click?*[11] discusses how colour affects clicking behaviour and there are multitudes of online articles discussing this in good depth.

An interesting addition to this is that button shape also matters. Bar and Neta[5] showed in 2006 that humans prefer curved visual objects.

Our own testing has typically confirmed this and many of our buttons are curved. We have found that the extent of the curvature may need to differ on different sites for optimal results.

Again, this depends on what else is visible on a page and how sympathetic the button is to its surroundings.

Best Practice Ten:
Trust factors and social proofs

One of the most important best practice techniques is to try to engender trust and credibility. This demonstrates the positive influence created when a person finds out that other people are having a positive experience. It makes them more likely to have a go themselves.

The sorts of things we look at are:

- Customer testimonials
- Short quotes from happy customers
- Case studies
- Embedded social media posts
- A metric like number of downloads or users
- Independent reviews
- Trust marks, certificate badges and associations

It is difficult to achieve but review/testimonial blocks should ideally have a photograph of the reviewer as well as a recent date, a name and company / role.

And, there should be a link to open a new window showing more on a third party, independent review site such as Trustpilot or Reviews.

Showing qualifications and awards can also showcase your talent and expertise.

Showing marks of authority help to reduce friction and anxiety, easing your users into an intellectual decision. They show that you take your industry seriously and have bought into known methods of validation.

And finally, a celebrity or industry leader endorsement can work in some cases. So good luck getting George Clooney to go on the record saying your brand is *bee's knees*.

Final thoughts.

Data-led Design® is about the intersection between the human and the data.

As marketers, we have become obsessed with the singular metrics that apparently signify success. And this has created a serious problem in how we understand what 'good' means in the long term.

Even within large, super-complex and high performing organisations. Narrow perspectives on what metrics matter are strife and steering decision making and growth in very limited and fragile directions.

To break out of this, we need to learn to value our opportunity and ability to observe human behaviours, desires and dislikes.

It's vital to break down the barrier between buyer and brand, and allowing yourself to reach out 'through the screen' and start meaningful and highly-intentional conversations with your website visitors.

When you bring together insights from

conversations, brought together data from tests, and data from tools. You begin to unlock decisions and a designs that bring about significant growth.

So, if you've reach the end of this short book, you've understood the ideas, and you've believed in the ethos that underpins the concepts of Data-Led Design®. You're next thing to do is act.

Transitioning to new ways of working can feel difficult and slow. So, start small.

Begin with introducing new tests. Tests which show you how people behave and what makes people click (on the right things).

The other next step is start changing your relationship with data and metrics. Especially metrics that you're only using because they look good in team meetings and monthly reports!

Let go of the numbers that just tell you that conversion is either going up or going down. And instead embrace the bring together of nuance and numbers, that paint a more truthful story of how people are really interacting with your brand.

Thank you for investing your time into this book and this model of working. I hope you can use what you have read to start making real change in how you drive results and bring humanity back into your marketing.

References

(1) https://www.sciencedaily.com/releases/2019/06/190605100345.htm
(2) https://biteable.com/blog/video-marketing-statistics/
(3) https://www.wyzowl.com/video-marketing-statistics-you-cant-ignore/#79%25 of people have been convinced to buy a piece of software or app after watching a brand%E2%80%99s video
(4) https://www.researchgate.net/publication/11293433_Eye contact detection in humans from birth

(5) (Bar, M., & Neta, M. (2006). Humans prefer curved visual objects. Psychological Science, 17(8), 645-648).

(6) https://journals.sagepub.com/doi/10.1111/j.1467-9280.2006.01759.x

(7) https://www.researchgate.net/publication/222285103 The influence of line spacing and text alignment on visual search of web pages

(8) https://en.wikipedia.org/wiki/Line_length -> Dyson, M. C., & Haselgrove, M. (2001).

(9) The influence of reading speed and line length on the effectiveness of reading from screen. International Journal of Human-Computer Studies, 54(4), 585-612

(10) https://cdn.shopify.com/s/files/1/0283/4667/9348/files/PS_VD01_Favourite_Pair_DESKTOP_reduced.mp4?v=1601622040

(11) Susan Weinschenk; *Neuro Web Design: What Makes Them Click*

(12) https://en.wikipedia.org/wiki/AIDA_(marketing)

(13) https://unbounce.com/conversion-rate-optimization/psychology-of-choice-conversion-rates/

(14) http://aei.pitt.edu/88182/

(15) http://psychclassics.yorku.ca/Miller/

(16) https://www.nngroup.com/articles/decision-framing-cognitive-bias-ux-pros/

(17) https://www.smashingmagazine.com/2017/10/avoid-bias-ux-feedback/

(18) https://econsultancy.com/research-shows-fewer-marketers-see-cro-as-crucial-in-2017-but-is-the-discipline-misunderstood/

(19) https://cxl.com/blog/2016-conversion-optimization-report/

(20) https://cxl.com/blog/2018-conversion-optimization-report/

(21) https://www.hubspot.com/marketing-statistics
(22) https://content.marketingsherpa.com/data/public/reports/special-reports/SR-Collected_Research_on_What_Really_Works_in_Optimization.pdf
(23) https://alrowe.co.uk/data-led-design-book-supporting-images/

Acknowledgements

I would like to thanks Matthew Hitches and Richard Chapman. Matthew Hitches was instrumental in the creation of Data-led Design® and this methodology. Richard Chapman also paved the way for this change in direction and several of the examples included in this book come from his work as a Conversion Rate Optimisation specialist. I would also like to thank Megan Carthy for her Support as well as the board of ClickThrough Marketing. Special thanks to Toby Moore for guiding the entire process and contributions to this edition of this book.

Data-led Design

The modern marketers guide to conversion rate optimisation.

By
Al Rowe

Printed in Great Britain
by Amazon

84719845R00058